worship BAND PLAY-ALONG

VOCAL EDITION *Volume 1*

Holy Is the Lord

Recorded and produced by Jim Reith at BeatHouse Music, Milwaukee, WI

Lead Vocals by Tonia Emrich and Jim Reith
Background Vocals by Jim Reith and Jana Wolf
Guitars by Mike DeRose
Bass by Chris Kringel
Piano by Kurt Cowling
Drums by Del Bennett

ISBN-13: 978-1-4234-1711-8
ISBN-10: 1-4234-1711-9

HAL•LEONARD® CORPORATION
7777 W. BLUEMOUND RD. P.O. BOX 13819 MILWAUKEE, WI 53213

Visit Hal Leonard Online at
www.halleonard.com

Holy Is the Lord

Agnus Dei

Words and Music by Michael W. Smith

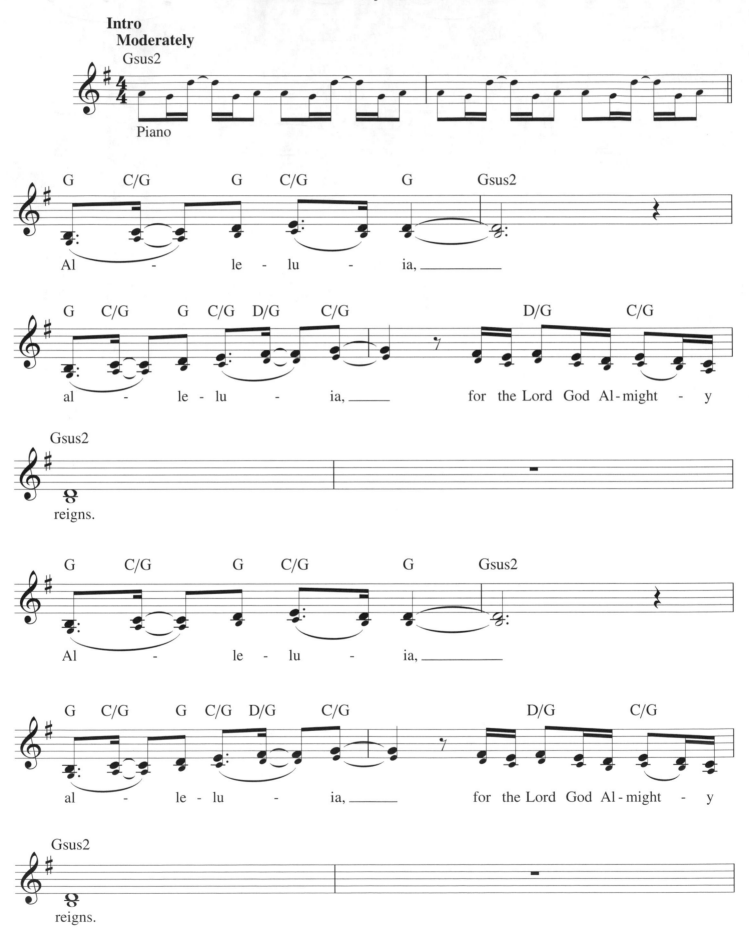

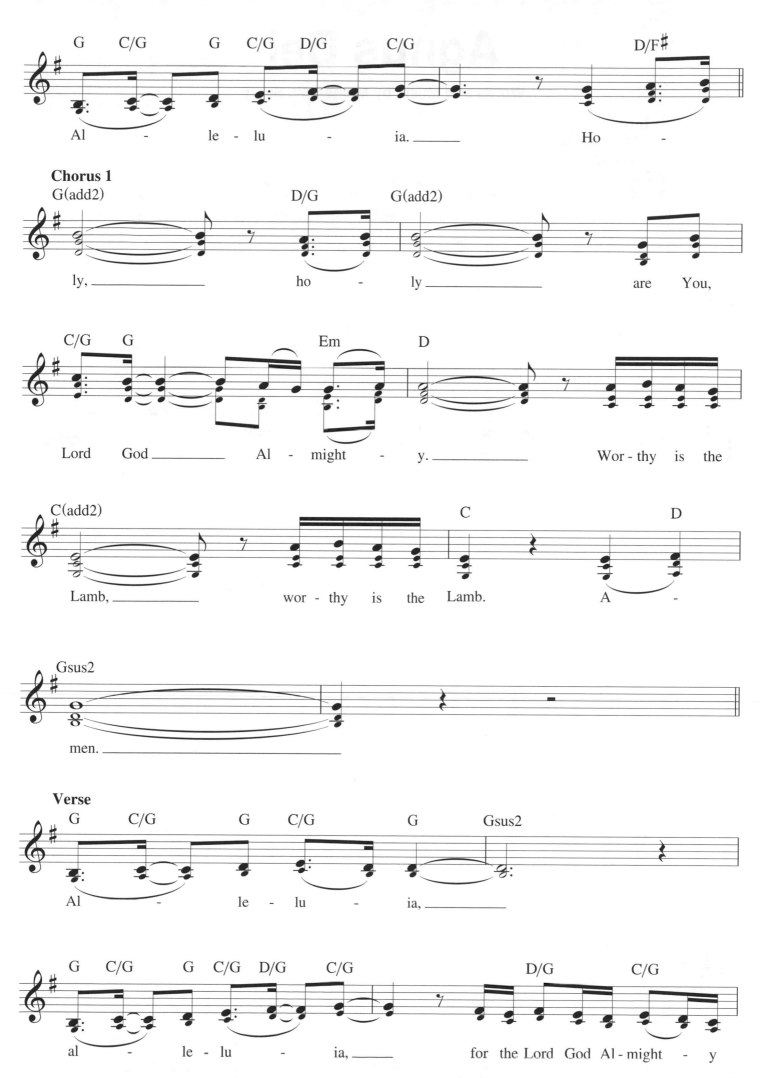

Chorus 1

Verse

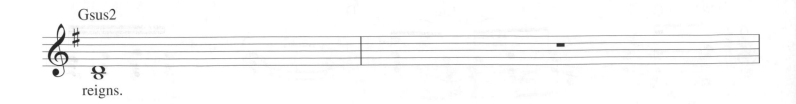

Gsus2

reigns.

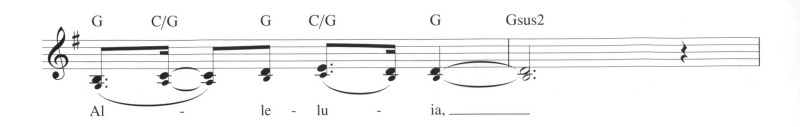

G　　C/G　　　　G　　C/G　　　　G　　　Gsus2

Al - le - lu - ia, _____

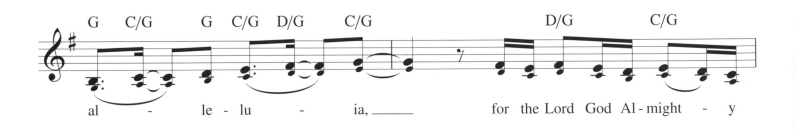

G　　C/G　　G　C/G　D/G　　C/G　　　　　　　D/G　　　　C/G

al - le - lu - ia, _____ for the Lord God Al - might - y

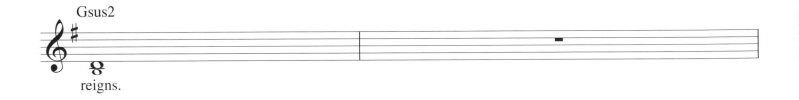

Gsus2

reigns.

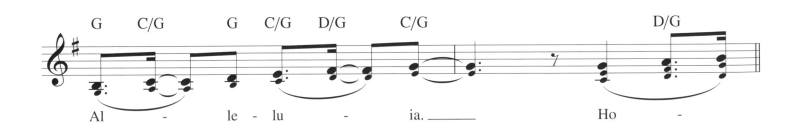

G　　C/G　　　G　　C/G　D/G　　　C/G　　　　　　　　D/G

Al - le - lu - ia. _____ Ho -

Chorus 2

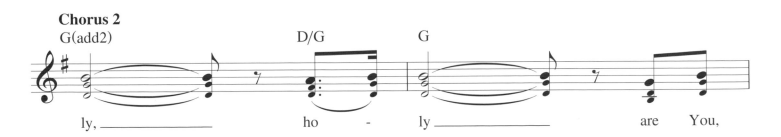

G(add2)　　　　　　　D/G　　　　G

ly, _____ ho - ly _____ are You,

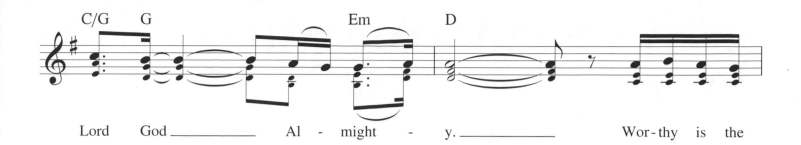

Lord God _____ Al - might - y. _____ Wor-thy is the

Lamb, _____ wor-thy is the Lamb. You are ho -

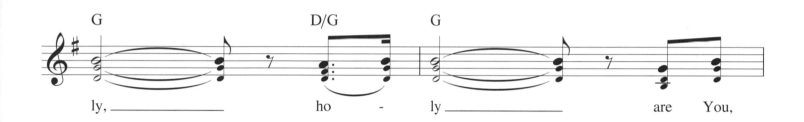

ly, _____ ho - ly _____ are You,

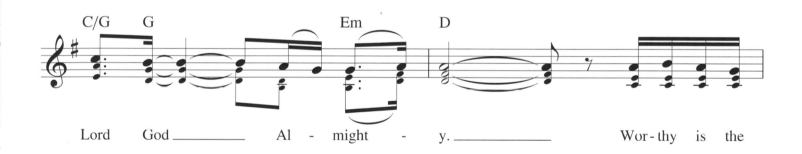

Lord God _____ Al - might - y. _____ Wor-thy is the

Lamb, _____ wor-thy is the Lamb. A -

men. _____

Be Unto Your Name

Words and Music by Lynn DeShazo and Gary Sadler

Intro
Moderately slow

Piano

Verse 1

We are a mo - ment, You are for - ev - er.

Lord of the ag - es, God be - fore time. ___

We are a va - por, You are e - ter - nal,

Love ev - er - last - ing, reign - ing on high. ___

Chorus

___ Ho - ly, ho - ly, Lord God Al - might -

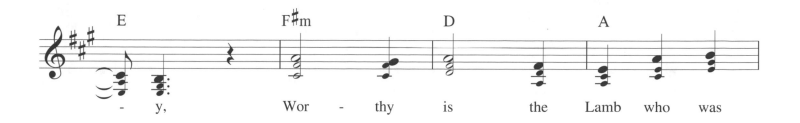

- y, Wor - thy is the Lamb who was

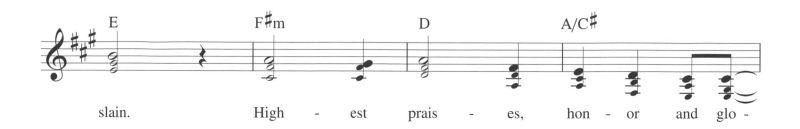

slain. High - est prais - es, hon - or and glo -

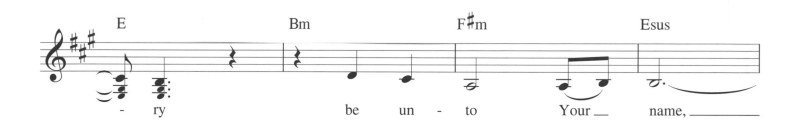

- ry be un - to Your __ name, _____

__ be un - to Your name. _____

Verse 2

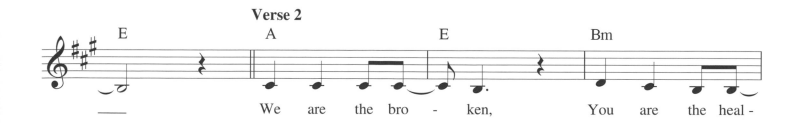

__ We are the bro - ken, You are the heal -

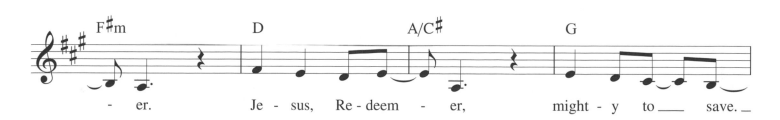

- er. Je - sus, Re - deem - er, might - y to __ save. _

You are the love _____ song we'll sing for - ev -

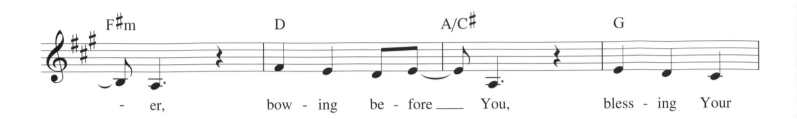

- er, bow - ing be - fore _____ You, bless - ing Your

Chorus

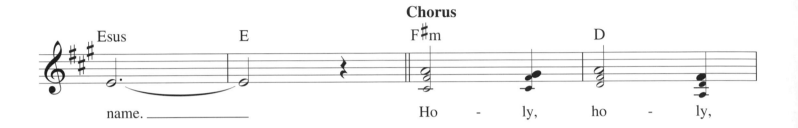

name. _____ Ho - ly, ho - ly,

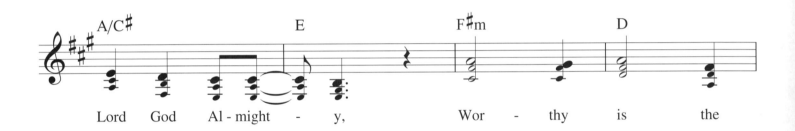

Lord God Al - might - y, Wor - thy is the

Lamb who was slain. High - est prais - es,

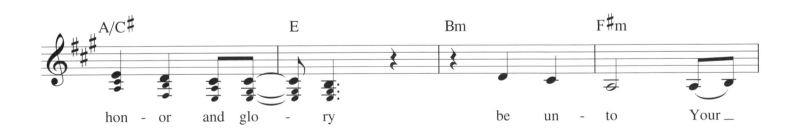

hon - or and glo - ry be un - to Your _____

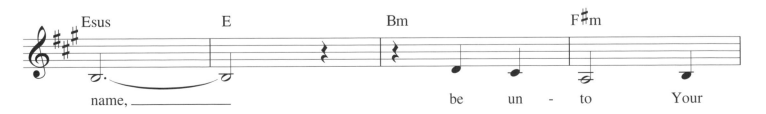

name, _____ be un - to Your

God of Wonders

Words and Music by Marc Byrd and Steve Hindalong

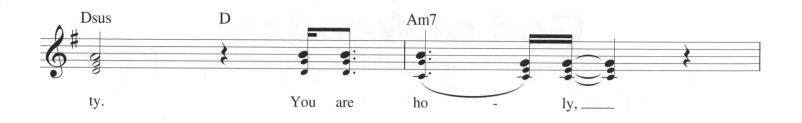

Dsus   D   Am7

ty.   You are ho - ly, ____

Csus2

ho - ly, ____   Lord of heav - en and ____ earth, ____

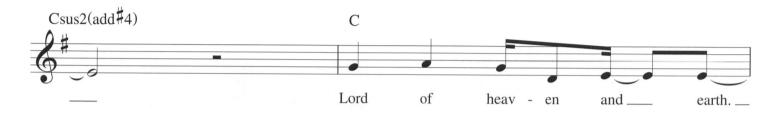

Csus2(add#4)   C

____ Lord of heav - en and ____ earth. ____

Verse 2

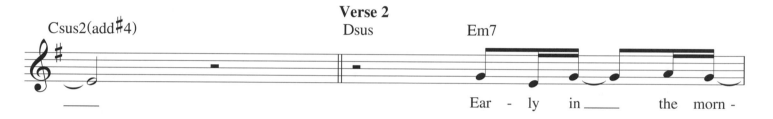

Csus2(add#4)   Dsus   Em7

____ Ear - ly in ____ the morn -

Csus2   Dsus   Em7

- ing ____   I will cel - e - brate ____ the ____

Csus2   Dsus   Em7

____ light. ____   And as I stum - ble in the dark -

C   Dsus   Em7

- ness, ____   I will call Your name ____ by ____

Csus2   **Chorus**
                    G

_____ night. _____ God of won - ders be - yond our gal - ax -

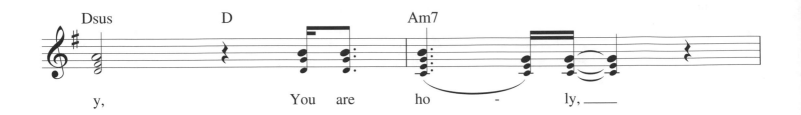

Dsus   D   Am7

y,   You are ho - ly, _____

Csus2   G

ho - ly. ___ The u - ni - verse __ de - clares Your maj - es -

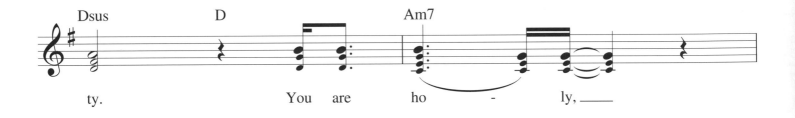

Dsus   D   Am7

ty.   You are ho - ly, _____

                        Bridge

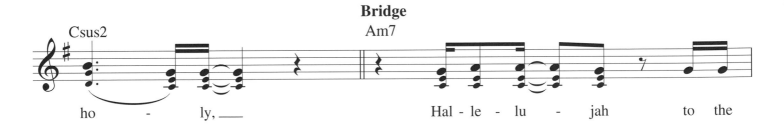

Csus2   Am7

ho - ly, ___ Hal - le - lu - jah to the

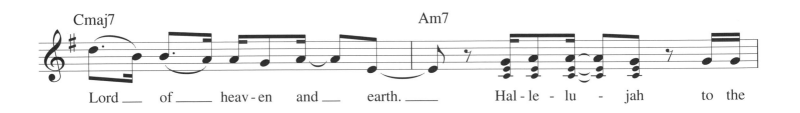

Cmaj7   Am7

Lord ___ of ___ heav - en and ___ earth. ___ Hal - le - lu - jah to the

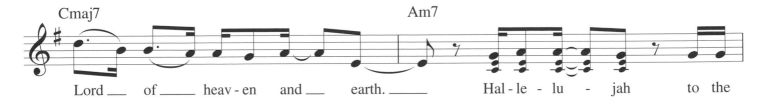

Cmaj7   Am7

Lord ___ of ___ heav - en and ___ earth. ___ Hal - le - lu - jah to the

Lord ___ of ___ heav - en and ___ earth. ___ Hal - le - lu - jah to the

Lord ___ of ___ heav - en and ___ earth. ___

Chorus

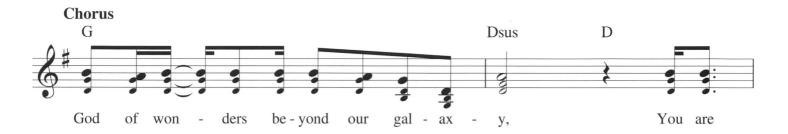

God of won - ders be - yond our gal - ax - y, You are

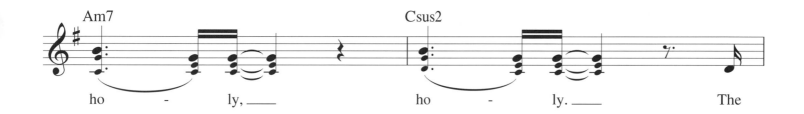

ho - ly, ___ ho - ly. ___ The

u - ni - verse ___ de - clares ___ Your maj - es - ty. You are

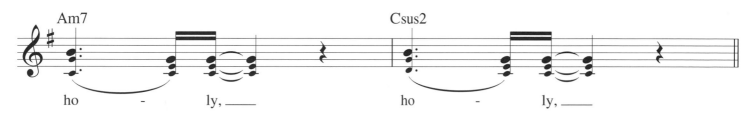

ho - ly, ___ ho - ly, ___

Chorus

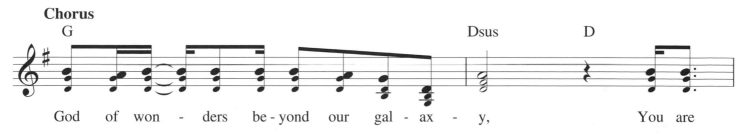

God of won - ders be - yond our gal - ax - y, You are

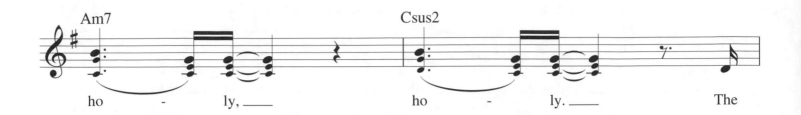

ho - ly, _____ ho - ly. _____ The

u - ni - verse _ de - clares _ Your maj - es - ty. You are

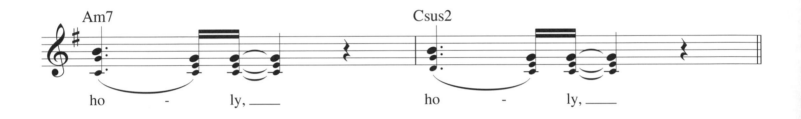

ho - ly, _____ ho - ly, _____

Outro

Lord of heav - en and ___ earth, _____

Lord of heav - en and ___ earth, _____

Lord of heav - en and ___ earth. _____

It Is You

Words and Music by Peter Furler

Intro
Moderately slow

Drum Fill   Piano

Verse

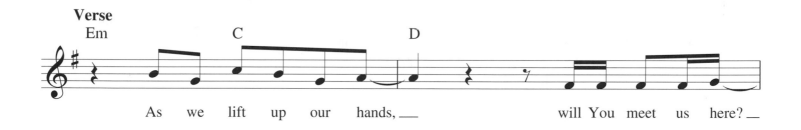

As we lift up our hands, ___ will You meet us here? ___

___ As we call on Your name, ___ will You meet us here? ___

___ We have come to this place ___ to wor - ship You, ___

___ God of mer - cy and ___ grace. ___ It is You ___

Pre-Chorus

____ we a - dore. _____ It is You __

____ prais - es are for. _____ On - ly You __

____ the heav - ens de - clare. ____ It is You, __

____ it is You. _____

Chorus

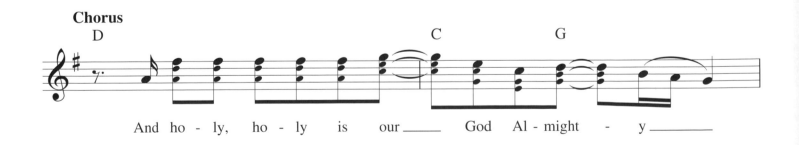

And ho - ly, ho - ly is our ____ God Al - might - y _____

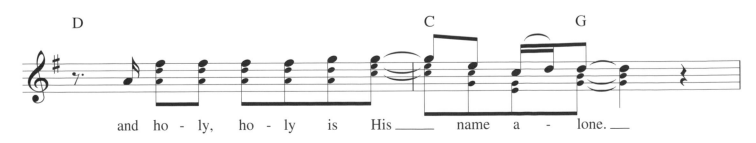

and ho - ly, ho - ly is His ____ name a - lone. __

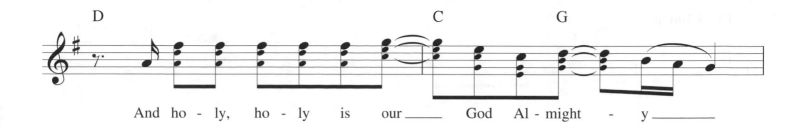

And ho - ly, ho - ly is our ____ God Al - might - y ____

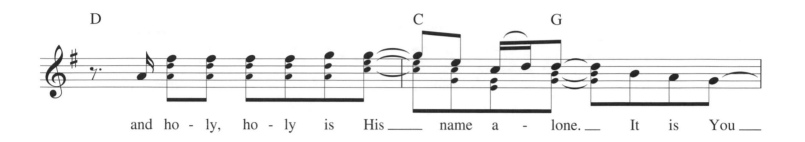

and ho - ly, ho - ly is His ____ name a - lone. ___ It is You ___

___ we a - dore. ____ It is You, ___

___ on - ly ___ You. _____

Verse

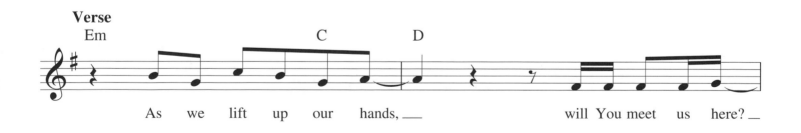

As we lift up our hands, ___ will You meet us here? __

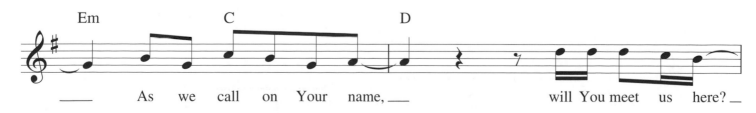

___ As we call on Your name, ___ will You meet us here? __

Em   C   D

___ We have come to this place ___ to wor - ship You, ___

Em   C   D

___ God of mer - cy and ___ grace. ___ It is You ___

Pre-Chorus

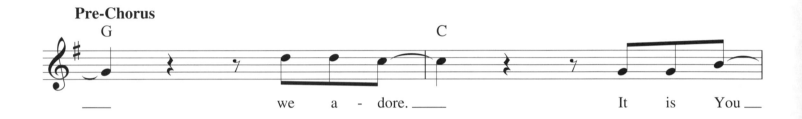

G   C

___ we a - dore. ___ It is You ___

G   C

___ prais - es are for. ___ On - ly You ___

G   C

___ the heav - ens de - clare. ___ It is You, ___

G   C

___ it is You. ___

Chorus

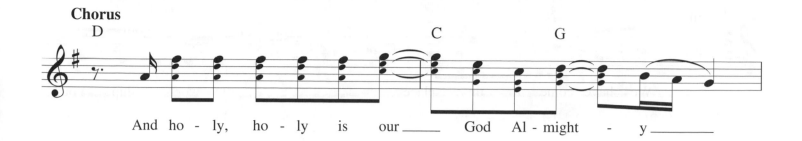

And ho - ly, ho - ly is our _____ God Al - might - y _____

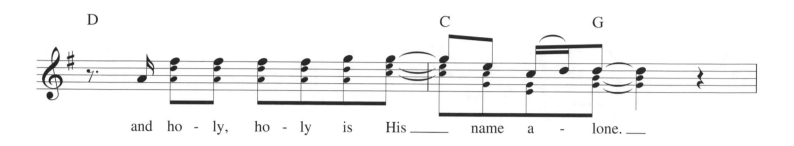

and ho - ly, ho - ly is His _____ name a - lone. _____

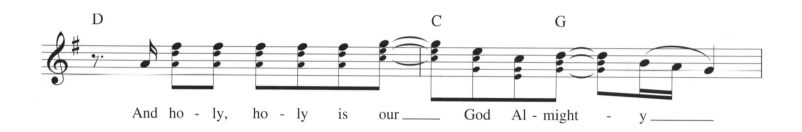

And ho - ly, ho - ly is our _____ God Al - might - y _____

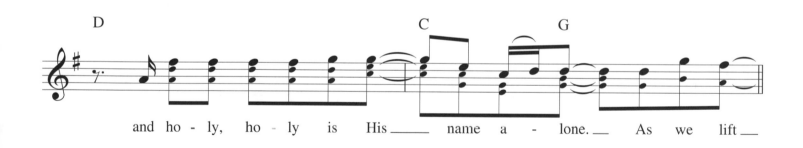

and ho - ly, ho - ly is His _____ name a - lone. _____ As we lift _____

Bridge

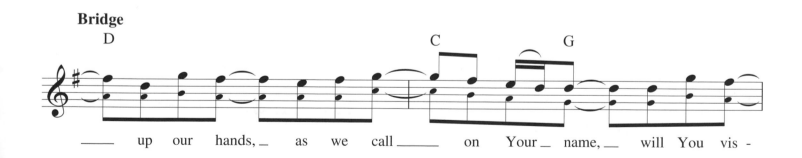

_____ up our hands, _ as we call _____ on Your _ name, _ will You vis -

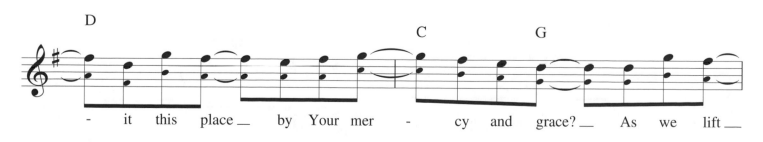

- it this place _ by Your mer - cy and grace? _ As we lift _____

up our hands, _ as we call ____ on Your _ name, _ will You vis -

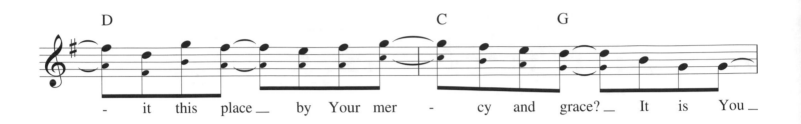

- it this place _ by Your mer - cy and grace? _ It is You _

___ we a - dore. ____ It is You, ___

___ it is You. _____

Chorus

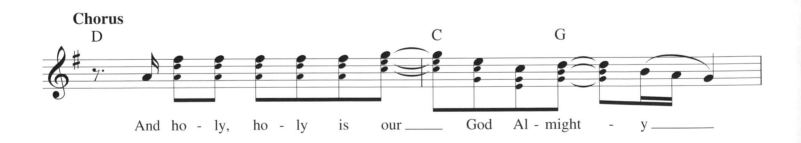

And ho - ly, ho - ly is our ____ God Al - might - y _____

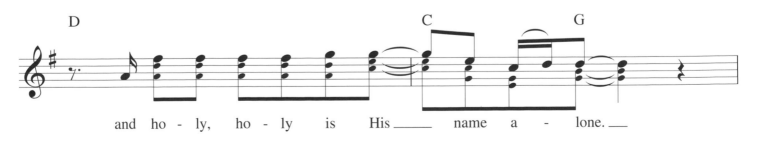

and ho - ly, ho - ly is His ____ name a - lone. _

22

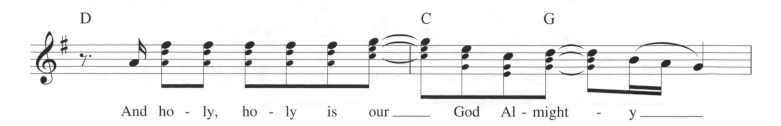

And ho - ly, ho - ly is our ___ God Al - might - y ___

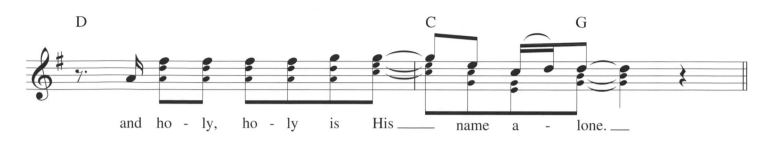

and ho - ly, ho - ly is His ___ name a - lone. ___

Chorus

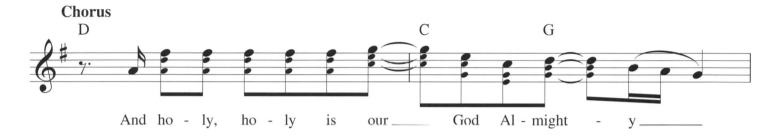

And ho - ly, ho - ly is our ___ God Al - might - y ___

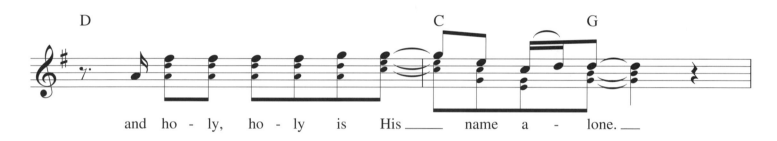

and ho - ly, ho - ly is His ___ name a - lone. ___

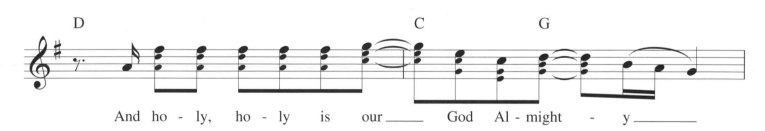

And ho - ly, ho - ly is our ___ God Al - might - y ___

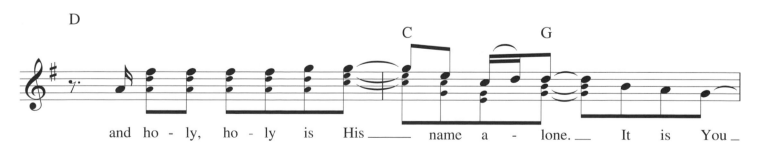

and ho - ly, ho - ly is His ___ name a - lone. ___ It is You ___

___ we a - dore. ___ It is You, ___ on - ly You. ___

Holy Is the Lord

Words and Music by Chris Tomlin and Louie Giglio

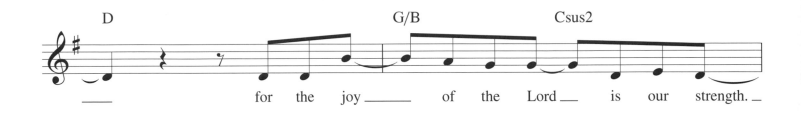

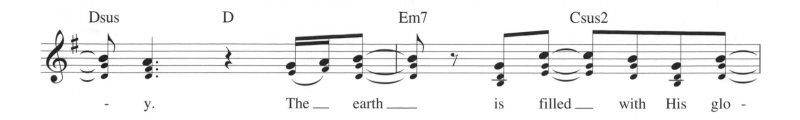

-y. The __ earth ___ is filled __ with His glo-

-ry. Ho-ly is the Lord __ God _____ Al might-

-y. The __ earth ___ is filled __ with His glo-

-ry, the __ earth ___ is filled __ with His glo-

Verse

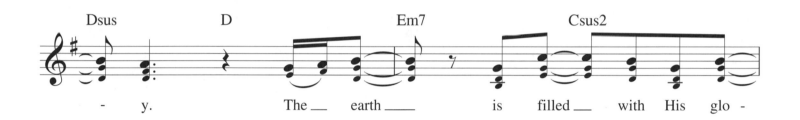

-ry. _____ We stand and lift up our hands _

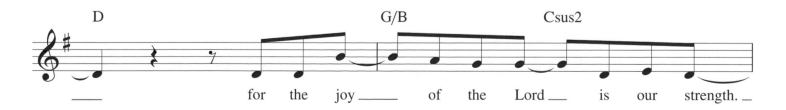

____ for the joy ___ of the Lord __ is our strength. _

| D | | G | | Csus2 | |

_____ We bow down _____ and wor -

| D | | | Em7 | Csus2 | |

- ship Him now. _____ How _ great, _____ how awe - some is He. _____

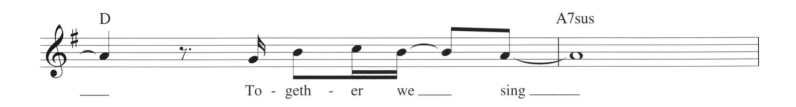

| D | | | A7sus | |

_____ To - geth - er we _____ sing _____

Chorus

| Csus2 | | G/B | | Csus2 | |

Ho - ly is the Lord _____ God _____ Al - might -

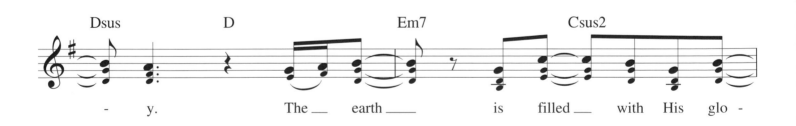

| Dsus | D | | Em7 | Csus2 | |

- y. The _ earth _____ is filled _ with His glo -

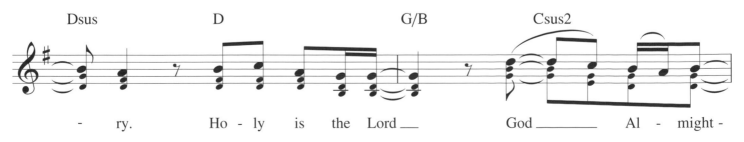

| Dsus | D | | G/B | Csus2 | |

- ry. Ho - ly is the Lord _____ God _____ Al - might -

Dsus   D   Em7   Csus2

- y.   The __ earth ___ is filled __ with His glo -

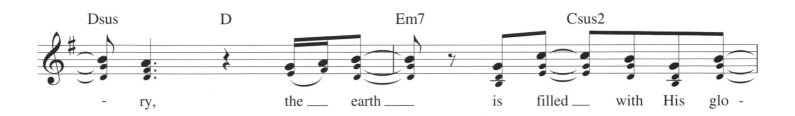

Dsus   D   Em7   Csus2

- ry,   the __ earth ___ is filled __ with His glo -

Bridge

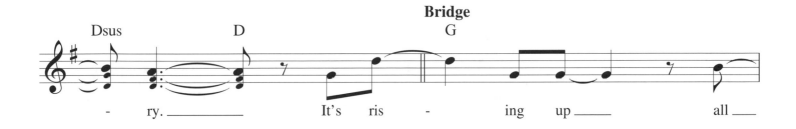

Dsus   D   G

- ry. _____ It's ris - ing up __ all __

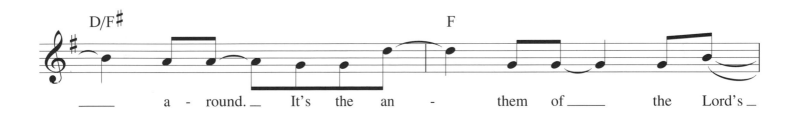

D/F#   F

_____ a - round. __ It's the an - them of __ the Lord's _

C   G

_____ re - nown. __ It's ris - ing up __ all __

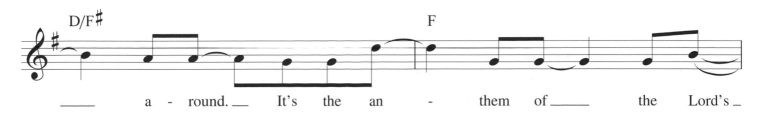

D/F#   F

_____ a - round. __ It's the an - them of __ the Lord's _

_re - nown. ___ And to - geth - er we ___ sing. ___

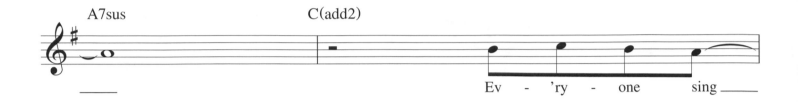

A7sus   C(add2)

_____ Ev - 'ry - one sing _____

A7sus   C(add2)   N.C.

_____ Ho - ly is the Lord ___

Chorus

G   C(add2)   D

___ God _____ Al - might - y. The ___ earth ___

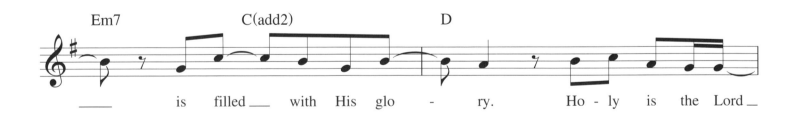

Em7   C(add2)   D

_____ is filled ___ with His glo - ry. Ho - ly is the Lord ___

G   C(add2)   D

_____ God _____ Al - might - y. The ___ earth ___

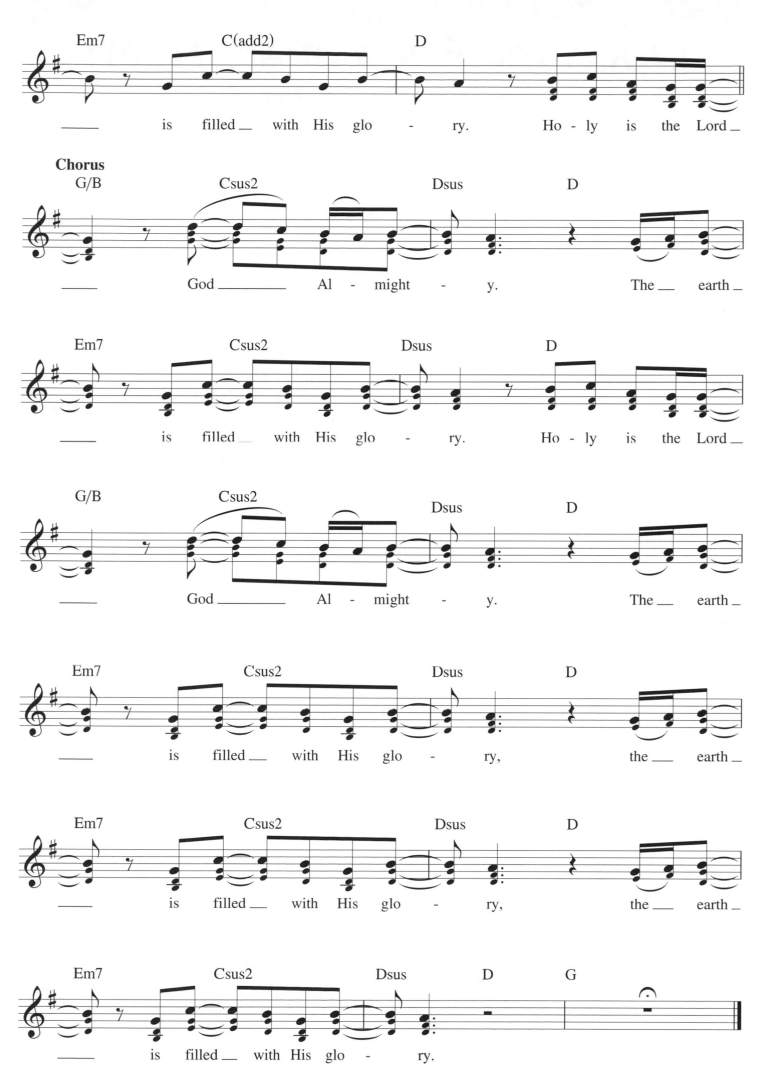

Chorus

29

Open the Eyes of My Heart

Words and Music by Paul Baloche

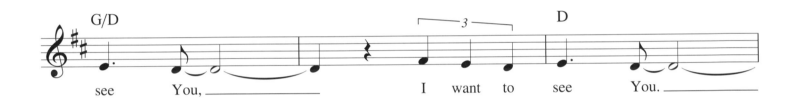

Chorus

high and lift - ed up, shin - ing in the light of Your glo -

- ry. Pour out Your pow - er and love as we sing

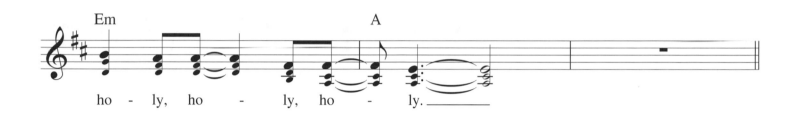

ho - ly, ho - ly, ho - ly.

Verse

O - pen the eyes ___ of my heart, ___ Lord. ___ O - pen the eyes ___ of my heart. ___

___ I want to see You, ___ I want to

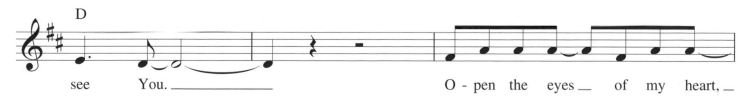

see You. ___ O - pen the eyes ___ of my heart, ___

Lord. ___ O - pen the eyes ___ of my heart. ___ I want to

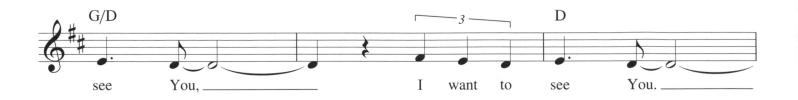

see You, _____ I want to see You. ___

Chorus

___ To see You high and lift - ed up, shin -

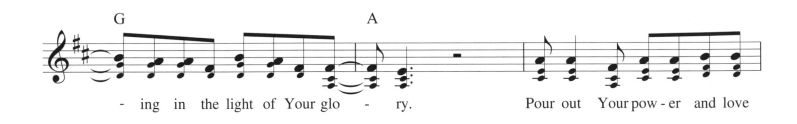

- ing in the light of Your glo - ry. Pour out Your pow - er and love

as we sing ho - ly, ho - ly, ho - ly. To see You

Chorus

high and lift - ed up, shin - ing in the light of Your glo -

-ry. Pour out Your pow - er and love

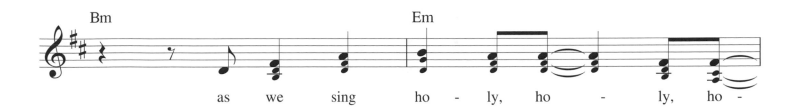

as we sing ho - ly, ho - ly, ho -

- ly. _____

Verse

Ho - ly, ho - ly, ho - ly, _____

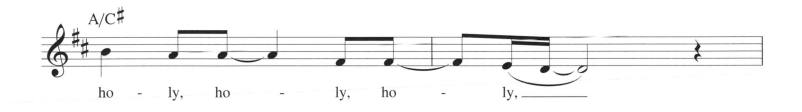

ho - ly, ho - ly, ho - ly, _____

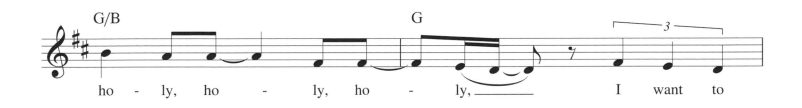

ho - ly, ho - ly, ho - ly, _____ I want to

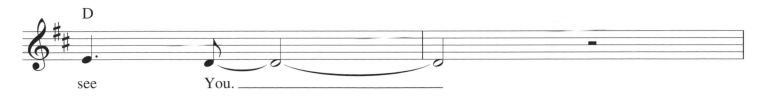

see You. _____

Ho - ly, ho - ly, ho - ly, _____

ho - ly, ho - ly, ho - ly, _____

ho - ly, ho - ly, ho - ly, _____ I want to

see You. _____ I want to

Tag

see You, _____ I want to

see You, _____ I want to see You, _ oh, _____

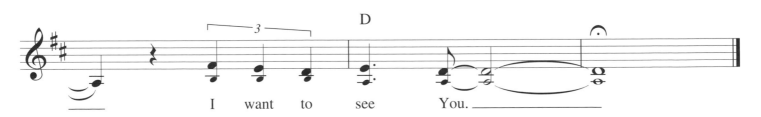

_____ I want to see You. _____

You Are Holy
(Prince of Peace)

Words and Music by Marc Imboden and Tammi Rhoton

Intro
With energy

Drum Fill   Piano

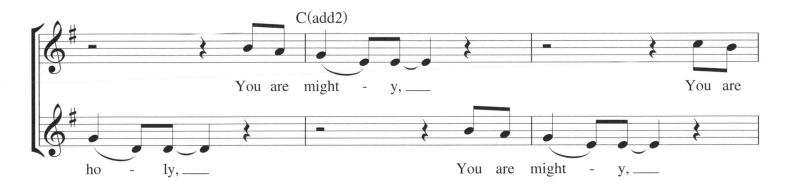

I will fol - low, ___ I will

praise. I will fol - low, ___

lis - ten, ___ I will love ___ You ___

I will lis - ten, ___ I will

all of my days. I will

love ___ You ___ all of my days. You are

Chorus

sing ___ to ___ and wor - ship ___ the King ___ who is

Lord of ___ lords, _ You are King of ___ kings, _ You are Might - y ___ God, _ Lord of

wor - thy. And I will love ___ and ___ a - dore ___ Him, ___ and I will

ev - 'ry - thing. You're Em - man - u - el, ___ You're the Great I ___ AM, ___ You're the

bow ___ down _ be - fore _____ Him. And I will sing ___ to ___ and

Prince of ___ Peace _ who _ is ___ the _Lamb. You're the Liv - ing _ God, _ You're my

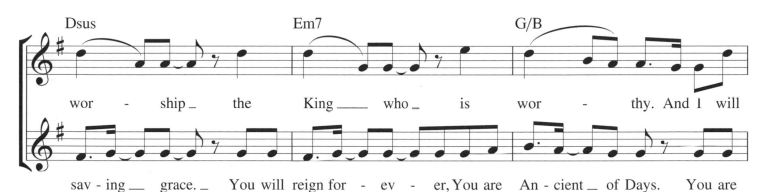

wor - ship _ the King _____ who _ is wor - thy. And I will

sav - ing _ grace. _ You will reign for - ev - er, You are An - cient _ of Days. You are

love ___ and _ a - dore ___ Him, _ and I will bow ___ down _ be -

Al - pha, O - me - ga, Be - gin - ning _ and _End. You're my Sav - ior, Mes - si - ah, Re-

fore _____ Him. You're my Prince of ___ Peace, _ and I will live my _ life for

deem - er _____ and _Friend. You're my Prince of ___ Peace, _ and I will live my _ life for

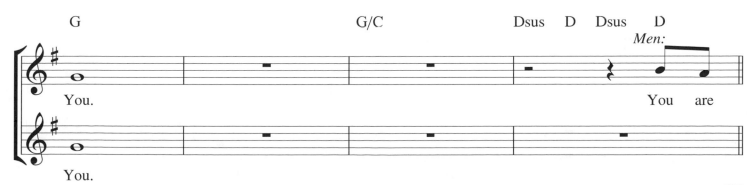

You. You are

You.

Chorus

We Fall Down

Words and Music by Chris Tomlin

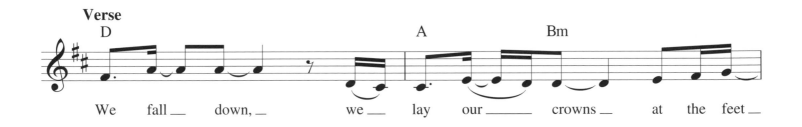

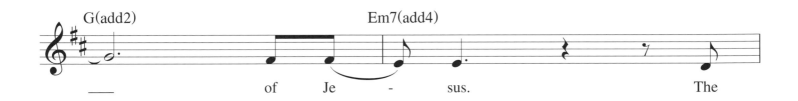

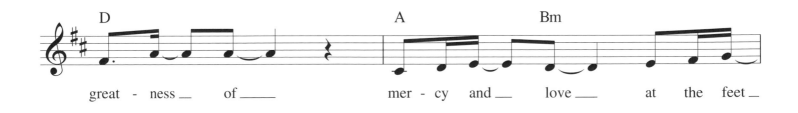

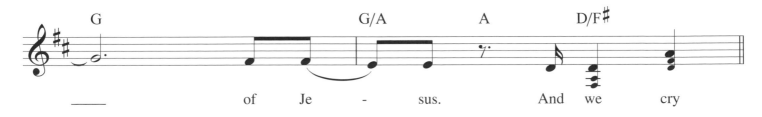

ho - ly, ho - ly, ho - ly. We cry

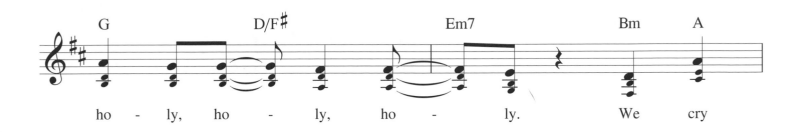

ho - ly, ho - ly, ho - ly. We cry

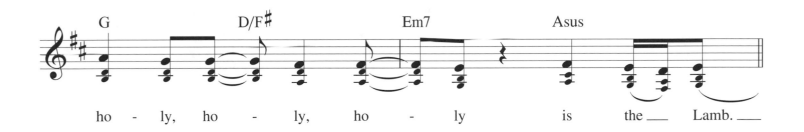

ho - ly, ho - ly, ho - ly is the ___ Lamb. ___

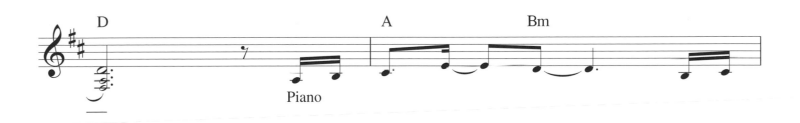

Piano

Verse

We fall ___ down, ___ we ___ lay our ___ crowns ___ at the feet ___

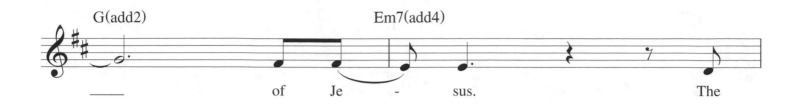

____ of Je - sus._ The

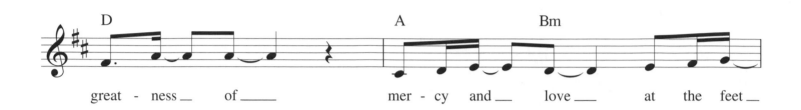

great - ness __ of ____ mer - cy and __ love __ at the feet __

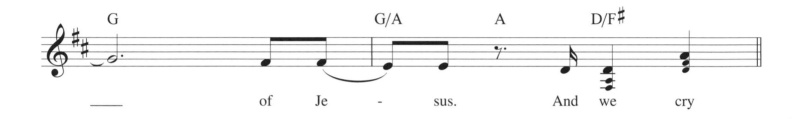

____ of Je - sus. And we cry

Chorus

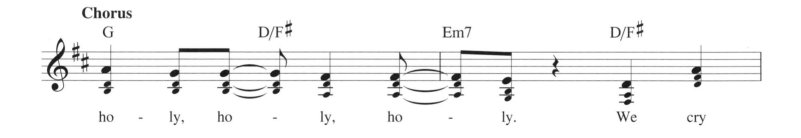

ho - ly, ho - ly, ho - ly. We cry

ho - ly, ho - ly, ho - ly. We cry

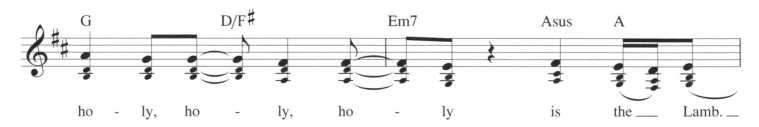

ho - ly, ho - ly, ho - ly is the __ Lamb. __

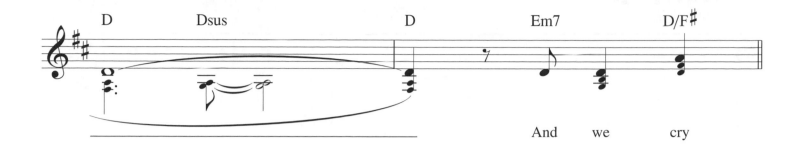

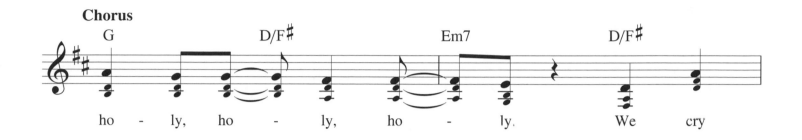

Chorus

ho - ly, ho - ly, ho - ly. We cry

ho - ly, ho - ly, ho - ly. We cry

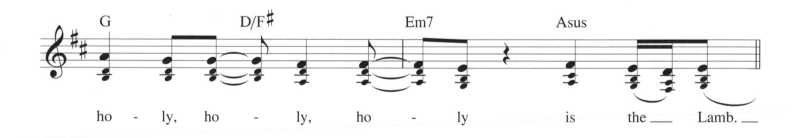

ho - ly, ho - ly, ho - ly is the __ Lamb. __

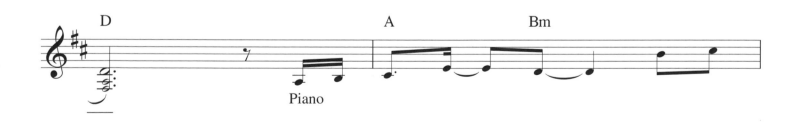

Piano

AGNUS DEI
MICHAEL W. SMITH

Key of **G Major**, 4/4

VERSE:

Gsus2 G   C/G G   C/G   G
     Al - le - lu - ia

G   C/G   G   C/G   D/G   C/G
Al - le - lu - ia

       D/G   **C/G G**
For the Lord God Almighty reigns

G   C/G   G   C/G   G
Al - le - lu - ia

G   C/G   G   C/G   D/G   C/G
Al - le - lu - ia

       D/G   **C/G G**
For the Lord God Almighty reigns

G   C/G   G   C/G   D/G   C/G
Al - le - lu - ia

CHORUS 1:

C/G   D/F♯   G
Ho - ly

D/F♯   G(add2)
Ho - ly

      C/G   G   Em   D
Are You, Lord God Almight - y

     C(add2)
Worthy is the Lamb

     C
Worthy is the Lamb

C   D   Gsus2
A - men

(REPEAT VERSE)

CHORUS 2:

C/E   D/G   G
Ho - ly

D/G   G
Ho - ly

      C/G   G   Em   D
Are You, Lord God Almight - y

     C(add2)
Worthy is the Lamb

     C(add2)
Worthy is the Lamb

     G
You are ho - ly

D/G   G
Ho - ly

      C/G   G   Em   D
Are You, Lord God Almight - y

     C
Worthy is the Lamb

     C
Worthy is the Lamb

C   D   Gsus2
A - men

BE UNTO YOUR NAME

LYNN DESHAZO and GARY SADLER

Key of **A Major, 3/4**

INTRO:

A E Bm F#m D Asus A Esus E

VERSE 1:

A   E   Bm   F#m
We are a moment, You are forever

D   A/C#   G   E
Lord of the ages,   God before time

A   E   Bm   F#m
We are a vapor, You are eternal

D   A/C#   G   Esus   E
Love everlasting, reigning on high

CHORUS:

F#m   D   A/C#   A
Holy, Holy, Lord God Almighty

F#m   D   A   E
Worthy is the Lamb who was slain

F#m   D   A/C#   E
Highest praises, honor and glory

Bm   F#m   Esus   E
    Be unto Your name

Bm   F#m   Esus   E
    Be unto Your name

VERSE 2:

A   E   Bm   F#m
We are the broken, You are the healer

D   A/C#   G   E
Jesus, Redeemer, mighty to save

A   E   Bm   F#m
You are the love song we'll sing forever

D   A/C#   G   Esus   E
Bowing before You, blessing Your name.

(REPEAT CHORUS 2X)

TAG:

Bm   F#m   Esus   E
    Be unto   Your name

Bm   F#m   Esus   E (hold)
    Be unto   Your name

GOD OF WONDERS

MARC BYRD and STEVE HINDALONG

Key of **G Major, 4/4**

VERSE 1:

Dsus Em7   Csus2
Lord of all creation

Dsus   Em   Csus2
Of water, earth and sky

Dsus   Em   Csus2
The heavens are Your tabernacle

Dsus   Em   Csus2
Glory to the Lord on high

CHORUS:

G   Dsus D
God of wonders beyond our galaxy

        Am7 Csus2
You are holy,   holy

     G   Dsus D
The universe declares Your majesty

        Am7 Csus2
You are holy,   holy

Csus2   Csus2(add#4)
Lord of heaven and earth

C   Csus2(add#4)
Lord of heaven and earth

VERSE 2:

Dsus Em7   Csus2
Early in the morning

Dsus   Em   Csus2
I will celebrate the light

Dsus Em7   C
And as I stumble in the darkness

Dsus   Em7   Csus2
I will call Your name by night

(REPEAT CHORUS)

BRIDGE:

Am7   Cmaj7
Hallelujah to the Lord of heaven and earth

Am7   Cmaj7
Hallelujah to the Lord of heaven and earth

Am7   Cmaj7
Hallelujah to the Lord of heaven and earth

Am7   Cmaj7
Hallelujah to the Lord of heaven and earth

Dsus   D

CHORUS:

G   Dsus D
God of wonders beyond our galaxy

        Am7 Csus2
You are holy,   holy

     G   Dsus D
The universe declares Your majesty

        Am7 Csus2
You are holy,   holy

Csus2   Csus2(add#4)
Lord of heaven and earth

C   Csus2(add#4)
Lord of heaven and earthC

C(add2)   Csus2(add#4)
Lord of heaven and earth

HOLY IS THE LORD

CHRIS TOMLIN and LOUIE GIGLIO

Key of **G Major**, 4/4

INTRO (GUITAR ONLY):

G Csus2 D

G Csus2 D

VERSE:

G   Csus2   D
We stand and lift up our hands

      G/B   Csus2   D
For the joy of the Lord is our strength

G   Csus2   D
We bow down and worship Him now

G/B   Csus2   D
How great, how awesome is He

         A7sus   Csus2
Together we sing

CHORUS:

        G/B Csus2 Dsus D
Holy is the Lord God Almighty

   Em7 Csus2   Dsus
The earth is filled with His glory

D   G/B Csus2 Dsus D
Holy is the Lord God Almighty

   Em7 Csus2   Dsus D
The earth is filled with His glory

   Em7 Csus2   Dsus D
The earth is filled with His glory

(REPEAT VERSE & CHORUS)

BRIDGE:

     G   D/F♯
It's rising up all around

           F   C
It's the anthem of the Lord's renown

     G   D/F♯
It's rising up all around

           F   C
It's the anthem of the Lord's renown

                 A7sus   Cadd2
And together we sing

           A7sus   Cadd2
Everyone sing

(REPEAT CHORUS)

(REPEAT LAST LINE OF CHORUS)

END ON G

IT IS YOU

PETER FURLER

Key of **G Major**, 4/4

INTRO:

Em C D   Em C D

VERSE:

Em   C   D
As we lift up our hands, will You meet us here
Em   C   D
As we call on Your name, will You meet us here
Em   C   D
We have come to this place to worship You
Em   C   D
God of mercy and grace

PRE-CHORUS:

     G   C
It is You we adore
     G   C
It is You praises are for
       G   C
Only You the heavens declare
     G   C
It is You, it is You

CHORUS:

D   C   G
And holy, holy is our God Almighty
D   C   G
And holy, holy is His name alone
D   C   G
And holy, holy is our God Almighty
D   C   G
And holy, holy is His name alone

TRANSITION BACK TO VERSE:

     G   C
It is You we adore
       G   C
It is You, only You

(REPEAT VERSE, PRE-CHORUS & CHORUS)

BRIDGE:

G   D
As we lift up our hands
         C   G
As we call on Your name
            D
Will You visit this place
         C   G
By Your mercy and grace
       D
As we lift up our hands
         C   G
As we call on Your name
           D
Will You visit in this place
         C   G
By Your mercy and grace
G   C
It is You we adore
     G   C
It is You, it is You

(REPEAT CHORUS 2X)

ENDING:

     G   C
It is You we adore
     G   C (hold)
It is You, only You

OPEN THE EYES OF MY HEART

PAUL BALOCHE

Key of **D Major**, 4/4

INTRO (FOUR BARS):

Dsus2

VERSE:

D
Open the eyes of my heart, Lord

A/D
Open the eyes of my heart

   G/D
I want to see You

   D
I want to see You

(REPEAT VERSE)

CHORUS:

   A   **Bm**
To see You high and lifted up

G   **A**
Shining in the light of Your glory

A   **Bm**
Pour out Your power and love

   G **A**
As we sing holy, holy, holy

(REPEAT VERSE 2X)

(REPEAT CHORUS 2X)

VERSE (2X):

D
Holy, holy holy

A/C♯
Holy, holy, holy

G/B   **G**
Holy, holy, holy

      D
I want to see You

TAG (2X):

D/F♯   **G**   **D**
I want to see You, I want to see You

WE FALL DOWN

CHRIS TOMLIN

Key of **D Major**, 4/4

INTRO (FOUR BARS):

D   A Bm G(add2)

VERSE:

D   A   Bm
We fall down, we lay our crowns

     G   Em7(add4)
At the feet of Jesus

     D   A   Bm
The greatness of mercy and love

     G   G/A A
At the feet of Jesus

CHORUS:

    D/F♯   G   D/F♯ Em7
And we cry holy, holy, holy

D/F♯   G   D/F♯ Em7
We cry holy, holy, holy

Bm A G   D/F♯ Em7
We cry holy, holy, holy

Asus D Dsus A Bm
Is the Lamb

G(add2) Em7(add4)

(REPEAT VERSE)

CHORUS:

    D/F♯   G   D/F♯ Em7
And we cry holy, holy, holy

D/F♯   G   D/F♯ Em7
We cry holy, holy, holy

Bm A G   D/F♯ Em7
We cry holy, holy, holy

Asus A D   Dsus D
Is   the Lamb

CHORUS:

Em7   D/F♯ G   D/F♯ Em7
And we cry   holy, holy, holy

D/F♯   G   D/F♯ Em7
We cry holy, holy, holy

Bm A G   D/F♯ Em7
We cry holy, holy, holy

Asus A D
Is   the Lamb

A Bm G Asus A D

YOU ARE HOLY (PRINCE OF PEACE)

MARC IMBODEN and TAMMI RHOTON

Key of **G Major**, 4/4

INTRO (EIGHT BARS):

G   G/C   Dsus D Dsus2 D

G   G/C   Dsus D Dsus2 D

VERSE:

    G(add2)   *Echo:*
You are holy   (*You are holy*)

    C(add2)
You are mighty   (*You are mighty*)

   Am7
You are worthy   (*You are worthy*)

    D
Worthy of praise (*worthy of praise*)

   G(add2)
I will follow   (*I will follow*)

   C(add2)2
I will listen   (*I will listen*)

    Am7
I will love You   (*I will love You*)

D   **G**   **D**   **G**
All of my days (*all of my days*)

CHORUS
(Part I and Part II sung simultaneously):

PART I

   Csus2   **Dsus**
I will sing to and worship

   Em7   **G/B**
The King who is worthy

    Csus2   **Dsus**
And I will love and adore Him

    Em7   **G/B**
And I will bow down before Him

    Csus2   **Dsus**
And I will sing to and worship

   Em7   **G/B**
The King who is worthy

    Csus2   **Dsus**
And I will love and adore Him

   Em7   **Asus** **A**
And I will bow down before Him

    C(add2)
You're my Prince of Peace

    D   **G**
And I will live my life for You.

(REPEAT VERSE)

(REPEAT CHORUS 2X)

TAG:

    Csus2
You're my Prince of Peace

    D   **G**
And I will live my life for You

PART II

    Csus2   **Dsus**
You are Lord of lords, You are King of kings

   Em7   **G/B**
You are mighty God, Lord of everything

    Csus2   **D**
You're Emmanuel, You're the Great I AM

   Em7   **G/B**
You're the Prince of Peace, who is the Lamb

    Csus2   **Dsus**
You're the Living God, You're my saving grace

   Em7   **G/B**
You will reign forever, You are Ancient of Days

    Csus2   **Dsus**
You are Alpha, Omega, Beginning and End

    Em7   **Asus**   **A**
You're my Savior, Messiah, Redeemer and Friend

    C(add2)
You're my Prince of Peace

    D   **G**
And I will live my life for You

THE SINGER'S MUSICAL THEATRE ANTHOLOGY

THE WORLD'S MOST TRUSTED SOURCE FOR GREAT THEATRE LITERATURE FOR SINGING ACTORS

Compiled and Edited by Richard Walters

The songs in this series are vocal essentials from classic and contemporary shows – ideal for the auditioning, practicing or performing vocalist. Each of the eighteen books contains songs chosen because of their appropriateness to that particular voice type. All selections are in their authentic form, excerpted from the original vocal scores. Each volume features notes about the shows and songs. There is no duplication between volumes.

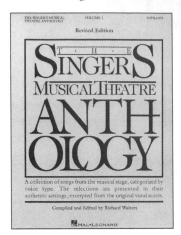

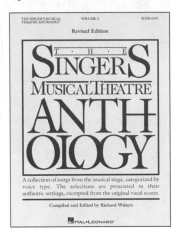

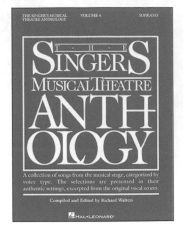

VOLUME 1

SOPRANO
(REVISED EDITION)

47 songs: Where or When • If I Loved You • Goodnight, My Someone • My Funny Valentine • Smoke Gets in Your Eyes • Barbara Song • Till There Was You • Falling in Love with Love • I Could Have Danced All Night • and many more.
00361071 Book Only $19.95
00740227 2 Accompaniment CDs...$22.95

MEZZO-SOPRANO/BELTER
(REVISED EDITION)

39 songs: Anyone Can Whistle • Broadway Baby • Doin' What Comes Naturally • Don't Cry for Me Argentina • Don't Tell Mama • How Are Things in Glocca Morra • Losing My Mind • Send in the Clowns • and more.
00361072 Book Only $19.95
00740230 2 Accompaniment CDs...$22.95

TENOR
(REVISED EDITION)

40 songs: Being Alive • Johanna • King Herod's Song • Stranger in Paradise • On the Street Where You Live • Younger Than Springtime • Lonely House • Not While I'm Around • Wish You Were Here • and more.
00361073 Book Only $19.95
00740233 2 Accompaniment CDs...$22.95

BARITONE/BASS
(REVISED EDITION)

39 songs: Camelot • C'est Moi • September Song • The Impossible Dream • Lonely Room • Marian the Librarian • Ol' Man River • Soliloquy • Some Enchanted Evening • and more.
00361074 Book Only $19.95
00740236 2 Accompaniment CDs...$22.95

DUETS

21 songs: Too Many Mornings • We Kiss in a Shadow • People Will Say We're in Love • Bess You Is My Woman • Make Believe • more.
00361075 Book Only $17.95
00740239 2 Accompaniment CDs...$22.95

VOLUME 2

SOPRANO
(REVISED EDITION)

42 songs: And This Is My Beloved • How Could I Ever Know • If I Were a Bell • Moonfall • I'll Know • Take Me to the World • The Sound of Music • Unusual Way • Warm All Over • and more.
00747066 Book Only $19.95
00740228 2 Accompaniment CDs...$22.95

MEZZO-SOPRANO/BELTER
(REVISED EDITION)

38 songs: You're the Top • The Party's Over • Adelaide's Lament • I Dreamed a Dream • As Long as He Needs Me • On My Own • I Can Cook Too • If He Walked Into My Life • Never Never Land • Small World • Tell Me on a Sunday • and more.
00747031 Book Only $19.95
00740231 2 Accompaniment CDs...$22.95

TENOR

42 songs: Miracles of Miracles • Sit Down, You're Rockin' the Boat • Bring Him Home • Music of the Night • Close Every Door • All Good Gifts • Anthem • I Belive In You • This Is the Moment • Willkommen • Alone at the Drive-In Movie.
00747032 Book Only $19.95
00740234 2 Accompaniment CDs...$22.95

BARITONE/BASS

40 songs: This Can't Be Love • Bye, Bye Baby • The Surrey with the Fringe on Top • Empty Chairs at Empty Tables • I've Grown Accustomed to Her Face • Stars • My Defenses Are Down • and more.
00747033 Book Only $19.95
00740237 2 Accompaniment CDs...$22.95

DUETS

30 duets, including songs from *Aida, Cabaret, Chicago, Guys and Dolls, Hairspray, The Last Five Years, The Phantom of the Opera, The Producers, Show Boat, Spamalot, Wicked* and more.
00740331 Book Only $19.95
00740240 2 Accompaniment CDs...$22.95

VOLUME 3

SOPRANO

40 songs: Getting to Know You • In My Life • My Favorite Things • Once You Lose Your Heart • Someone to Watch over Me • Think of Me • Whistle Down the Wind • Wishing You Were Somehow Here Again • Wouldn't It Be Loverly • and more.
00740122 Book Only $19.95
00740229 2 Accompaniment CDs...$22.95

MEZZO SOPRANO/BELTER

41 songs: As If We Never Said Goodbye • But Not for Me • Everything's Coming up Roses • I Ain't Down Yet • Maybe This Time • My Heart Belongs to Daddy • Someone like You • Stepsisters' Lament • The Ladies Who Lunch • You Can't Get a Man with a Gun • many more.
00740123 Book Only $19.95
00740232 2 Accompaniment CDs...$22.95

TENOR

35 songs: Almost Like Being in Love • Any Dream Will Do • Corner of the Sky • Hey There • Mama Says • Mister Cellophane • One Song Glory • Steppin' Out with My Baby • Sunset Boulevard • What You'd Call a Dream • Your Eyes • and more.
00740124 Book Only $19.95
00740235 2 Accompaniment CDs...$22.95

BARITONE/BASS

42 songs: All I Care About • Gigi • I Confess • If I Can't Love Her • If I Sing • The Kid Inside • Les Poissons • Lucky to Be Me • Marry Me a Little • Paris by Night • Santa Fe • and more.
00740125 Book Only $19.95
00740238 2 Accompaniment CDs...$22.95

VOLUME 4

SOPRANO

40 songs: Bewitched • Children Will Listen • Home • I Have Dreamed • It's a Most Unusual Day • A Lovely Night • One Boy (Girl) • The Song Is You • Speak Low • We Kiss in a Shadow • Why Do I Love You? • Why Was I Born? • and more.
00000393 Book Only $19.95
00000397 2 Accompaniment CDs...$22.95

MEZZO SOPRANO/BELTER

37 songs: Anything but Lonely • Heaven Help My Heart • I Can Hear the Bells • I Don't Know How to Love Him • Just One Step • Life with Harold • The Man That Got Away • Popular • Roxie • Shadowland • There Are Worse Things I Could Do • The Wizard and I • and more.
00000394 Book Only $19.95
00000398 2 Accompaniment CDs...$22.95

TENOR

37 songs: Awaiting You • Dancing Through Life • Goodnight Saigon • If You Were Gay • Love Changes Everything • A Man Could Go Quite Mad • One Track Mind • Tschaikowsky (And Other Russians) • Who Am I? • You Walk with Me • and more.
00000395 Book Only $19.95
00000399 2 Accompaniment CDs...$22.95

BARITONE/BASS

40 songs: Along Came Bialy • Edelweiss • Get Me to the Church on Time • I'm Not Wearing Underwear Today • A Lot of Livin' to Do • Put on a Happy Face • Wonderful • Ya Got Trouble • and more.
00000396 Book Only $19.95
00000401 2 Accompaniment CDs...$22.95

Prices, contents, and availability are subject to change without notice.

Please visit www.halleonard.com for complete contents listings.

FOR MORE INFORMATION, SEE YOUR LOCAL MUSIC DEALER,
OR WRITE TO:

HAL•LEONARD®
CORPORATION
7777 W. BLUEMOUND RD. P.O. BOX 13819 MILWAUKEE, WI 53213

0107

pro Vocal®
BETTER THAN KARAOKE!

Pro Vocal® Series
Songbook & Sound-Alike CD
Sing 8 Chart-Topping Songs with a Professional Band

Whether you're a karaoke singer or an auditioning professional, the Pro Vocal® series is for you! Each book contains the lyrics, melody, and chord symbols for eight hit songs. The CD contains demos for listening, and separate backing tracks so you can sing along. The CD is playable on any CD player, but it is also enhanced so PC and Mac computer users can adjust the recording to any pitch without changing the tempo! Perfect for home rehearsal, parties, auditions, corporate events, and gigs without a backup band.

ELVIS PRESLEY – VOLUME 1
Blue Suede Shoes • Can't Help Falling in Love • Don't Be Cruel (To a Heart That's True) • Good Luck Charm • I Want You, I Need You, I Love You • Love Me • (Let Me Be Your) Teddy Bear • Treat Me Nice.
00740333 ....$14.95

BROADWAY SONGS
Women's Edition
A Change in Me (Beauty and the Beast) • I Can Hear the Bells (Hairspray) • Memory (Cats) • On My Own (Les Misérables) • Someone like You (Jekyll & Hyde) • There Are Worse Things I Could Do (Grease) • Without You (Rent).
00740247 ....$14.95

Men's Edition
Alone at the Drive-In Movie (Grease) • Any Dream Will Do (Joseph and the Amazing Technicolor® Dreamcoat) • Bring Him Home (Les Misérables) • Elaborate Lives (Aida) • Seasons of Love (Rent) • They Live in You (Disney Presents The Lion King: The Broadway Musical) • This Is the Moment (Jekyll & Hyde) • Why God Why? (Miss Saigon).
00740248 ....$14.95

CHRISTMAS STANDARDS
Each song is in the style of the artist listed.

Women's Edition
Frosty the Snow Man (Patti Page) • Let It Snow! Let It Snow! Let It Snow! (Lena Horne) • Merry Christmas, Darling (Carpenters) • My Favorite Things (Barbra Streisand) • Rockin' Around the Christmas Tree (Brenda Lee) • Rudolph the Red-Nosed Reindeer (Ella Fitzgerald) • Santa Baby (Eartha Kitt) • Santa Claus Is Comin' to Town (The Andrews Sisters).
00740299 ....$12.95

Men's Edition
Blue Christmas (Elvis Presley) • The Christmas Song (Chestnuts Roasting on an Open Fire) (Nat King Cole) • The Christmas Waltz (Frank Sinatra) • Here Comes Santa Claus (Right down Santa Claus Lane) (Gene Autry) • (There's No Place Like) Home for the Holidays (Perry Como) • I'll Be Home for Christmas (Bing Crosby) • Let It Snow! Let It Snow! Let It Snow! (Vaughn Monroe) • Silver Bells (Ray Conniff).
00740298 ....$14.95

CONTEMPORARY HITS
Women's Edition
Beautiful (Christina Aguilera) • Breathe (Faith Hill) • Complicated (Avril Lavigne) • Don't Know Why (Norah Jones) • Fallin' (Alicia Keys) • The Game of Love (Santana feat. Michelle Branch) • I Hope You Dance (Lee Ann Womack with Sons of the Desert) • My Heart Will Go On (Celine Dion).
00740246 ....$14.95

Men's Edition
Drive (Incubus) • Drops of Jupiter (Tell Me) (Train) • Fly Away (Lenny Kravitz) • Hanging by a Moment (Lifehouse) • Iris (Goo Goo Dolls) • Smooth (Santana feat. Rob Thomas) • 3 AM (Matchbox 20) • Wherever You Will Go (The Calling).
00740251 ....$14.95

DISCO FEVER
Women's Edition
Boogie Oogie Oogie (A Taste of Honey) • Funkytown (Lipps Inc.) • Hot Stuff (Donna Summer) • I Will Survive (Gloria Gaynor) • It's Raining Men (The Weather Girls) • Le Freak (Chic) • Turn the Beat Around (Vicki Sue Robinson) • We Are Family (Sister Sledge).
00740281 ....$12.95

Men's Edition
Boogie Fever (The Sylvers) • Da Ya Think I'm Sexy (Rod Stewart) • Get Down Tonight (KC and the Sunshine Band) • Love Rollercoaster (Ohio Players) • Stayin' Alive (The Bee Gees) • Super Freak (Rick James) • That's the Way (I Like It) (KC and the Sunshine Band) • Y.M.C.A. (Village People).
00740282 ....$12.95

'80s GOLD
Women's Edition
Call Me (Blondie) • Flashdance ... What a Feeling (Irene Cara) • Girls Just Want to Have Fun (Cyndi Lauper) • How Will I Know (Whitney Houston) • Material Girl (Madonna) • Mickey (Toni Basil) • Straight Up (Paula Abdul) • Walking on Sunshine (Katrina and the Waves).
00740277 ....$12.95

Men's Edition
Every Breath You Take (The Police) • Heart and Soul (Huey Lewis) • Hurts So Good (John "Cougar") • It's Still Rock and Roll to Me (Billy Joel) • Jessie's Girl (Rick Springfield) • Maneater (Hall & Oates) • Summer of '69 (Bryan Adams) • You Give Love a Bad Name (Bon Jovi).
00740278 ....$12.95

JAZZ STANDARDS
Great jazz classics, each in the style of the artist listed.

Women's Edition
Bye Bye Blackbird (Carmen McRae) • Come Rain or Come Shine (Judy Garland) • Fever (Peggy Lee) • The Girl from Ipanema (Astrud Gilberto) • Lullaby of Birdland (Ella Fitzgerald) • My Funny Valentine (Sarah Vaughan) • Stormy Weather (Keeps Rainin' All the Time) (Lena Horne) • Tenderly (Rosemary Clooney).
00740249 ....$14.95

Men's Edition
Ain't Misbehavin' (Louis Armstrong) • Don't Get Around Much Anymore (Tony Bennett) • Fly Me to the Moon (In Other Words) (Frank Sinatra) • Georgia on My Mind (Ray Charles) • I've Got You Under My Skin (Mel Torme) • Misty (Johnny Mathis) • My One and Only Love (Johnny Hartman) • Route 66 (Nat King Cole).
00740250 ....$14.95

Prices, contents, & availability subject to change without notice.

R&B SUPER HITS
Women's Edition
Baby Love (The Supremes) • Dancing in the Street (Martha & The Vandellas) • I'm So Excited (Pointer Sisters) • Lady Marmalade (Patty LaBelle) • Midnight Train to Georgia (Gladys Knight & The Pips) • Rescue Me (Fontella Bass) • Respect (Aretha Franklin) • What's Love Got to Do with It (Tina Turner).
00740279 ....$12.95

Men's Edition
Brick House (Commodores) • I Can't Help Myself (Sugar Pie, Honey Bunch) (The Four Tops) • I Got You (I Feel Good) (James Brown) • In the Midnight Hour (Wilson Pickett) • Let's Get It On (Marvin Gaye) • My Girl (The Temptations) • Shining Star (Earth, Wind & Fire) • Superstition (Stevie Wonder).
00740280 ....$12.95

WEDDING GEMS
Women's Edition
Grow Old with Me (Mary Chapin Carpenter) • How Beautiful (Twila Paris) • The Power of Love (Celine Dion) • Save the Best for Last (Vanessa Williams) • We've Only Just Begun (Carpenters) • When You Say Nothing at All (Alison Krauss & Union Station) • You Light up My Life (Debby Boone) • You Needed Me (Anne Murray).
00740309 Book/CD Pack $12.95

Men's Edition
Back at One (Brian McKnight) • Butterfly Kisses (Bob Carlisle) • Here and Now (Luther Vandross) • I Will Be Here (Steven Curtis Chapman) • In My Life (The Beatles) • The Keeper of the Stars (Tracy Byrd) • Longer (Dan Fogelberg) • You Raise Me Up (Josh Groban).
00740310 Book/CD Pack $12.95

Duets Edition
Don't Know Much (Aaron Neville & Linda Ronstadt) • Endless Love (Diana Ross & Lionel Richie) • From This Moment On (Shania Twain & Bryan White) • I Finally Found Someone (Barbra Streisand & Bryan Adams) • I Pledge My Love (Peaches & Herb) • Nobody Loves Me like You Do (Anne Murray & Dave Loggins) • Tonight, I Celebrate My Love (Peabo Bryson & Roberta Flack) • Up Where We Belong (Joe Cocker & Jennifer Warnes).
00740311 ....$12.95

ANDREW LLOYD WEBBER
Women's Edition
All I Ask of You • As If We Never Said Goodbye • Don't Cry for Me Argentina • I Don't Know How to Love Him • Memory • Unexpected Song • Wishing You Were Somehow Here Again • With One Look.
00740348 ....$14.95

Men's Edition
All I Ask of You • Any Dream Will Do • I Only Want to Say (Gethsemane) • Love Changes Everything • Memory • The Music of the Night • No Matter What • On This Night of a Thousand Stars.
00740349 ....$14.95